Table of  !

Meet Tim!

— Hi! I'm Tim. What's your name?
(Pause for the child to respond.)
— Oh, that's a cool name! Tell me, do you like to play? I LOVE playing! Cars, dinosaurs, hide-and-seek—I love everything!

(Tim holds up his hands.)
— But here's the problem... When I play, my hands get super messy! Look, there's a juice stain... and here's some paint! Oh, what's this? Oops... is that chocolate!

— Have your hands ever been messy? What did you do about it?
(Pause.)
— Wow, great idea! Hey, let's find out why we need to wash our hands!

2

3

Messy Hands, Clean Hands!

— Uh-oh! My hands are still messy! Look, there's chocolate here and some paint over there...

— Do your hands get messy too?

(Pause for child to answer.)

— What do you do when your hands are dirty?
(Pause for answer.)

— That's right! We need to wash them. But why?

4

— Whoa! Did you know there are tiny invisible germs on our hands?

— They can make us sick if we don't wash them away! Yikes!

6

Let's Wash Our Hands!

— Let's wash our hands together! First, turn on the water.

— Now, grab some soap! Rub, rub, rub!

— Sing along to the ABC song while you scrub!

9

-Look! My hands are clean now !

-High five!

10

-Uh-oh! Some sneaky little germs are

hiding here! Can you count how

many there are?

Point to each one and say the number out loud!

I found_____ germs!

12

Brushing Teeth is Fun!

— Do you know what I do every morning and

night? I brush my teeth!

— Do you brush your teeth too?

 (Pause for child to answer)

— That's awesome!

But do you know why we do it every day?

14

— Tiny little sugar bugs live on our teeth! If we don't brush, they throw a party in our mouths!

— And guess what? They don't like toothpaste!

16

Let's Brush Together!

First, put some toothpaste on your brush...

— Now, brush up and down, round and round!

— Don't forget the back teeth!

18

-Look! Now my teeth are super clean and shiny!

— Show me your biggest, brightest smile!

20

21

Help Tim find toothbrush!

- Oh no! Tim's toothbrush is lost! Can you help it

find its way to his teeth? Draw a line to connect

the toothbrush to Tim's big, shiny smile!

22

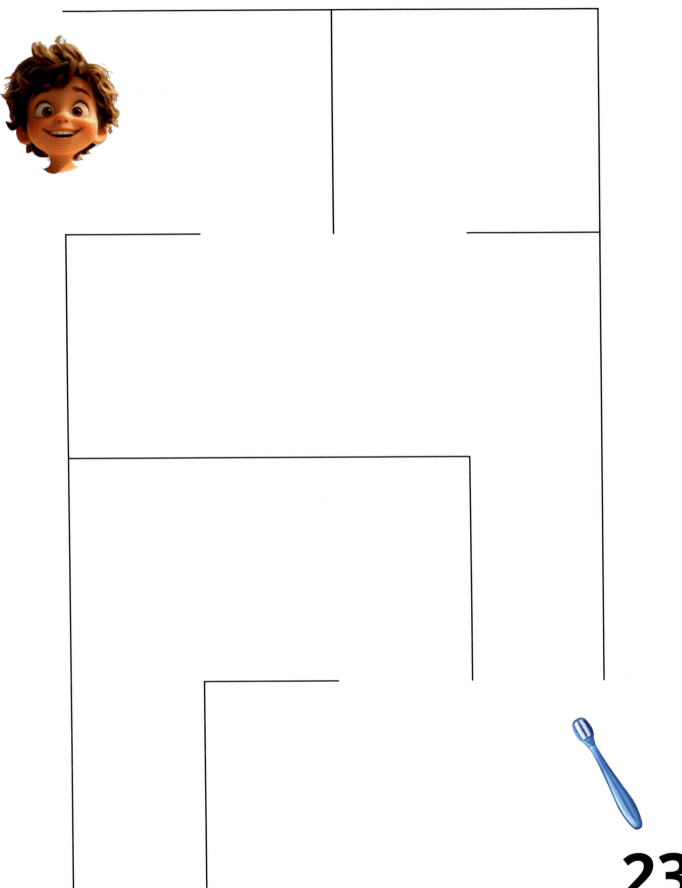

23

Why Do We Take a Bath?

- Whoa! Look at my feet! They're so dirty from playing outside!

— Do your feet ever get dirty too?

 (Pause for child to answer.)

— What should we do when we're all messy?

That's right—take a bath!

-Tiny little germs love to hide in the dirt!

— But guess what? They're afraid of soap and water!

Let's wash up!

-Let's wash up! First, let's splash some water...

— Now, grab the soap and scrub, scrub, scrub!

— Don't forget your toes! Wiggle, wiggle!

29

Ahhh! Now I'm fresh and clean!

— I smell so good! Sniff, sniff!

31

Help Tim Find the Words!

— Oh no! Some words are hiding in this puzzle! Can you help me find them?

— Let's ask Mom or Dad to help us. When you find a word, circle it!

BUBBLES

SOAP

SHAMPOO

TOWEL

"Great job! Now you're a real word-finding champion!"

32

```
K  W  R  A  A  O  I  J  Y  G  W  P  I  P
I  W  S  H  A  M  P  O  O  O  A  E  M  P
K  Q  W  O  T  S  E  I  N  L  J  M  W  A
C  Q  L  U  O  T  B  O  E  B  Q  M  B  V
C  F  B  R  L  D  O  B  V  G  W  F  U  B
O  C  L  Y  U  A  V  W  F  K  T  F  B  Q
N  A  J  F  N  D  J  M  T  D  P  E  B  N
P  O  N  I  Y  E  O  F  T  O  W  E  L  N
M  A  S  X  W  R  N  C  B  E  M  D  E  U
L  P  O  O  V  R  K  U  F  Q  C  P  S  F
E  H  A  C  P  A  F  A  F  M  N  H  E  J
W  E  P  N  F  P  P  Q  W  U  M  V  F  G
H  P  Y  W  E  A  S  T  U  G  J  V  U  Z
N  C  O  M  S  T  P  T  M  S  C  D  O  A
U  D  D  I  L  L  U  L  H  C  Q  I
```

33

Tim and the Dirty Shirt!

— Oh no! Look at my shirt! There's a big stain on it.
I think it's... ketchup? Or maybe mud?

— Have you ever gotten your clothes dirty while playing?

(Pause for child's response.)

— What should we do when our clothes get dirty?

(Pause for answer.)

— That's right! We need to wash them! But how? Let's find out!

34

I know! We need to wash it! But where do we wash clothes?

(Pause for child to answer.)

— That's right! In the washing machine! Let's put my shirt inside!

— What else do we need to make it clean?

(Pause for answer.)

— Soap and water! Now let's start the machine and watch it spin!

— Look! My shirt is all clean now! It smells so fresh!

(Sniffs shirt.)

— But wait... it's still wet! What should we do now?

(Pause for child to answer.)

— Hang it up? Great idea! Let's put it on the clothesline to dry!

38

39

My shirt is drying on the clothesline. But how long do we wait? One minute? Five minutes?

(Pause for child's guess.)

— Nooo, it takes longer! What can we do while we wait? Let's play a game!

41

My Shirt is Dry!

— Look! My shirt is dry now! It feels so warm from the sun!

(Tim takes the shirt off the clothesline and hugs it.)

— Should I put it on?

(Pause for child to answer.)

— Okay! Let's see... One arm in... now the other... and pull it down!

(Tim puts on his fresh, clean shirt.)

— Yay! Now I'm clean and ready to play again!

43

Color Tim's Clean Shirt!

-Tim washed his dirty shirt, and now it's fresh

and clean! Can you color his shirt and make it

look bright and happy?

44

45

Folding Fun with Tim!

— Phew! Now everything is clean! But... what should we do next?

— Hmm... What do you think? Where do we put clothes after washing them?

(Pause for the child to answer.)

— In the closet? Great idea! But first, let's fold them neatly!

(Tim picks up a T-shirt and shows it.)

— Look! First, we smooth it out... now fold the sleeves... then in half... Yay! Now it's nice and tidy!

— Let's try folding something else together!

46

47

Name the Colors!

— Wow! Look at this neatly folded stack of clothes! Can you name the colors of each layer? Let's try together!

(Pause for the child to respond.)

— Great! Let's say all the colors again from top to bottom! What color is the very top piece? And the next one?

(Pause for the child to respond.)

— Wow, you're amazing! Now you're a real color expert!

49

Tim's Big Closet Clean-Up

— Whoa! My closet looks like a tornado swept through it! My shirts are on the floor, my socks are playing hide and seek under the bed, and my pants are in a big messy pile.

— Do you think I can find my favorite red shirt in this mess? Let's see...

(Pause for the child to answer.)

— Hmm... Nope, not here! Maybe under the bed? Or... what if it's hiding behind the chair? Where should I check next?

(Pause for guesses.)

— Let's check together! Ready? On the count of three—one, two, three... let's look!

— Can you find something red around you right now? Maybe your socks, a toy, or even a book?

— Oh! I found my missing sock, but where's my shirt?

— Have you ever lost your clothes in a messy room?

(Pause for the child to answer.)

— What should we do to make our clothes easier to find?

(Pause for the child to answer.)

— That's right! We should fold them and put them away neatly! But first, I still have to find that red shirt... Let's keep looking!

53

— Oh no! I opened the drawer, and all the clothes spilled onto the floor! I guess it's really time to clean up...

— Where should I start? With shirts, socks, or pants?

(Pause for the child to answer.)

— Great idea! Let's start with the socks. Oh no, they're all mixed up! Can you help me find the matching pairs?

Draw a line to match the socks that look the same!"

54

55

— Great job! Now all the socks are in place.

— Now let's sort out the T-shirts! Here's my green one, here's my blue one... but where's my favorite red T-shirt?

(Pause for the child to answer.)

— That's right! It might be under the pile of clothes. Let's dig through it together!

57

— Yay! I found my favorite red shirt! Now my clothes won't get lost again.

— What do you think we should do to keep the room tidy?

(Pause for the child to answer.)

— That's right! Let's fold all the clothes neatly and put them away where they belong.

59

Help Tim Find His Way to Diner!

— Uh-oh! I'm so hungry! But I can't find my way to my plate... Can you help me?

(Pause for the child to respond.)

— Look! There are so many paths... but some of them lead to funny things! A rubber duck? A lost sock? I don't think I can eat those!

— Can you help me find the right path to my food? Try tracing it with your finger!

(Pause while the child follows the maze.)

— Yay! You did it! Now I can finally eat. Thank you for helping me! What's your favorite food?

(Pause for the child to answer.)

— That sounds delicious! Let's eat together!

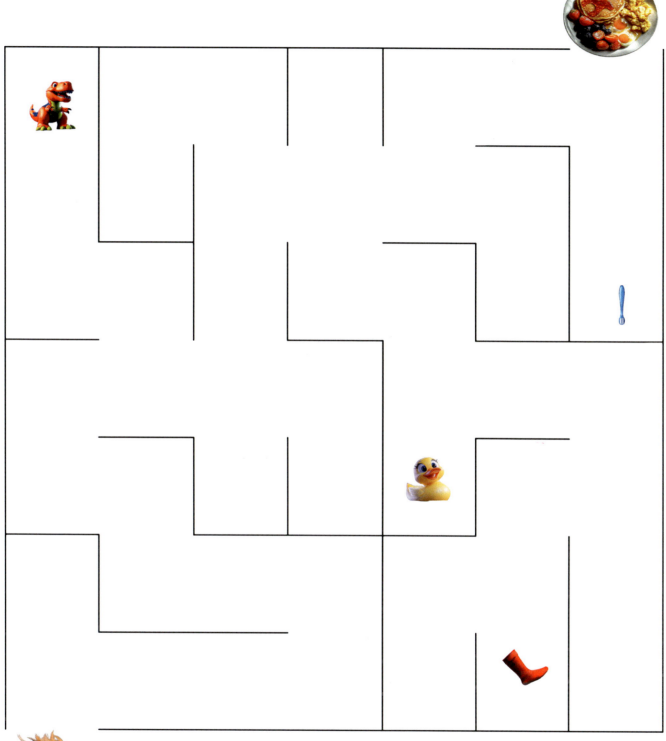

61

Pack the Backpack!

— Oh no! My backpack is empty! I need to pack it for the day. Can you help me?

(Pause for the child to respond.)

— Hmm... what do I need? A book? A toy? Maybe a sandwich? Let's find the right things to put inside!
— Look at all these items! Can you find what belongs in my backpack? Point to the things I should take with me!

(Pause for the child to choose.)

— Great job! Now my backpack is ready. What do you pack in your bag when you go out?

(Pause for the child to answer.)

— That sounds perfect! Now we're both ready for the day!

How Many Apples?

— Hi! It's me, Tim! Today, I have some apples. Look how beautiful they are!

— Let's count them together! How many apples do you see?

(Pause for the child to answer.)
— Great job! Let's count them together out loud-one, two, three, four, five, six!

— Wow! We have six apples! Can you tell me what colors they are?

(Pause for the child to answer.)

— That's right! We have red, yellow, and green apples. Great job! Now we know how many there are!

-Don't forget to wash your apples before eating – clean fruit keeps us healthy and happy!"

— Hi there! Look, I have a delicious apple! Do you like apples?

(Pause for the child to answer.)

— Apples are so yummy and good for you! What color do you think this apple is?

(Pause for the child to answer.)

— That's right! Apples can be red, green, or even yellow. What's your favorite color?

(Pause for the child to answer.)

— Great choice! Now, let's color this picture together! What color will you make my apple?

67

The End of Tim's Adventure!

— Wow! We did so many fun things together! We washed up, cleaned my room, and even found all my missing socks.

— Did you have fun?

(Pause for the child to answer.)

— I did too! And guess what? Now I feel happy and fresh.

— What was your favorite part of our adventure?
(Pause for the child to answer.)

— That sounds awesome! I'm so glad you helped me. Let's go on another adventure soon!

68

70

K	W	R	A	A	O	I	J	Y	G	W	P	I	P
I	W	S	H	A	M	P	O	O	O	A	E	M	P
K	Q	W	O	T	S	E	I	N	L	J	M	W	A
C	Q	L	U	O	T	B	O	E	B	Q	M	B	V
C	F	B	R	L	D	O	B	V	G	W	F	U	B
O	C	L	Y	U	A	V	W	F	K	T	F	B	Q
N	A	J	F	N	D	J	M	T	D	P	E	B	N
P	O	N	I	Y	E	O	F	T	O	W	E	L	N
M	A	S	X	W	R	N	C	B	E	M	D	E	U
L	P	O	O	V	R	K	U	F	Q	C	P	S	F
E	H	A	C	P	A	F	A	F	M	N	H	E	J
W	E	P	N	F	P	P	Q	W	U	M	V	F	G
H	P	Y	Y	W	E	A	S	T	U	G	J	V	

71

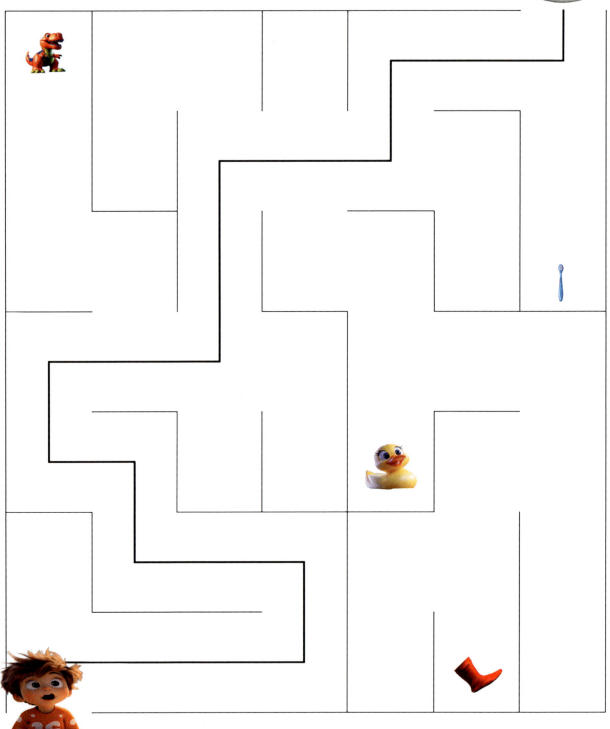

Made in United States
North Haven, CT
25 May 2025

69204965R00042